THE STORY OF RUBY BRIDGES

A Biography Book for New Readers

Written by
Arlisha Norwood, PhD

Illustrated by
Katie Crumpton

ROCKRIDGE PRESS

For my Family.

"If you know whence you came, there is really no limit to where you can go."
—James Baldwin

For general information on our other products and services or to obtain technical support, please contact our Customer Care Department within the United States at (866) 744-2665, or outside the United States at (510) 253-0500.

Rockridge Press publishes its books in a variety of electronic and print formats. Some content that appears in print may not be available in electronic books, and vice versa.

Series Designer: Angela Navarro
Interior and Cover Designer: Scott Petrower
Art Producer: Hannah Dickerson
Editor: Erum Khan
Production Editor: Ruth Sakata Corley
Production Manager: Martin Worthington

Illustrations © 2021 Katie Crumpton. Photography © Bettmann/Getty Images, p. 48; Underwood Archives/Getty Images, p. 50; Randy Duchaine/Alamy Stock Photo, p. 51. All maps used under license from Creative Market. Author photo courtesy of Jason A. Alston.

ISBN: Print 978-1-64876-539-1 | eBook 978-1-64876-540-7
R0
Printed in China

CONTENTS

CHAPTER 1

A BRAVE GIRL IS BORN

Meet Ruby Bridges

When Ruby Bridges was a child, she loved playing jacks and climbing trees. She loved playing with her neighbors and friends. She lived an ordinary life. This all changed when Ruby started the first grade. She became a **civil rights** leader!

In 1960, Ruby became the first African American student in the South to attend an all-white school. Although you probably attend school with all kinds of different children, this was not the case in the 1950s and 1960s. Black and white children went to **segregated** schools. They did not play in the same parks, or even swim in the same pools. In fact, Black people and white people did everything separately. Black Americans were treated unfairly and often faced **violence** if they chose not to follow the rules of segregation.

Ruby faced danger attending her new school, but she remained determined. Ruby did not let others sway her from her path. As an adult, Ruby has continued to work to end **racism**. Today, she is a famous **activist** who speaks out about **injustice**. Ruby's bold actions changed the course of history.

In the next few pages, you will learn about Ruby's life. You will learn about her childhood, her family, and her community.

You will learn about what inspired her, how she conquered her fears, and how she approached difficulties and barriers. You will learn how she was brave.

People around the world have been inspired by Ruby's story. It reminds people to speak out when they see things that are wrong. It shows that it is possible to overcome fears.

Ruby's story shows that one little girl can change the world.

JUMP IN THE THINK TANK

When you hear the words "brave," "courageous," and "strong," who do you think of? Do you picture a family member, neighbor, or maybe someone from school? Think of someone who inspires you to be brave.

Ruby's America

Ruby Bridges was born in 1954 in Tylertown, Mississippi. When she was growing up, the world was very different from the one we are in today. Ruby and other African Americans were treated badly because of their skin color.

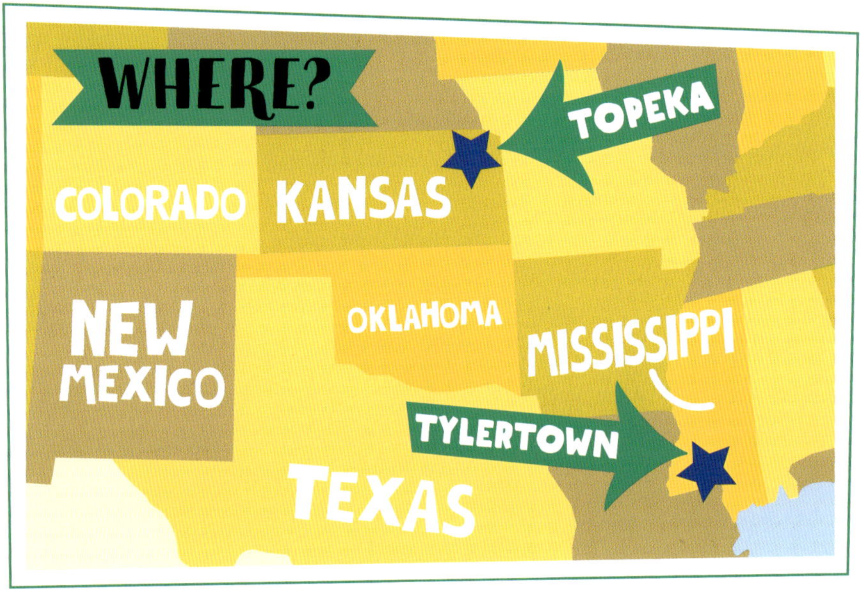

Most places were segregated, which meant that Black people and white people were kept separate. They could not eat in the same restaurants, go to the same movie theaters, or even play at the same parks. These rules applied to schools, too.

During the same year that Ruby was born, a group of African American parents in Topeka, Kansas, decided to go to court. They wanted to challenge the law that said schools should be segregated. The case made it all the way to the **Supreme Court**, the highest court in the country. The nine judges ruled that segregated public schools were **unconstitutional**. This ruling meant that every public school in the United States had to allow white children and Black children to learn together. The case came to be known as *Brown v. Board of Education*. Although the Supreme Court made segregation in schools illegal, many schools in the South still refused to allow Black students to attend.

This was the world that Ruby grew up in. Although she faced **discrimination** and segregation, Ruby's family raised her with a lot of joy and love. For the most part, as a child she did not even realize that her life was segregated. In 1960, this all changed.

> "My world in those days was comfortable and safe."

WHEN?

MAY 17, 1954
The Supreme Court rules to desegregate schools.

SEPTEMBER 8, 1954
Ruby is born.

DECEMBER 1955
The Montgomery Bus Boycott begins.

DECEMBER 1956
The boycott ends and public buses are desegregated.

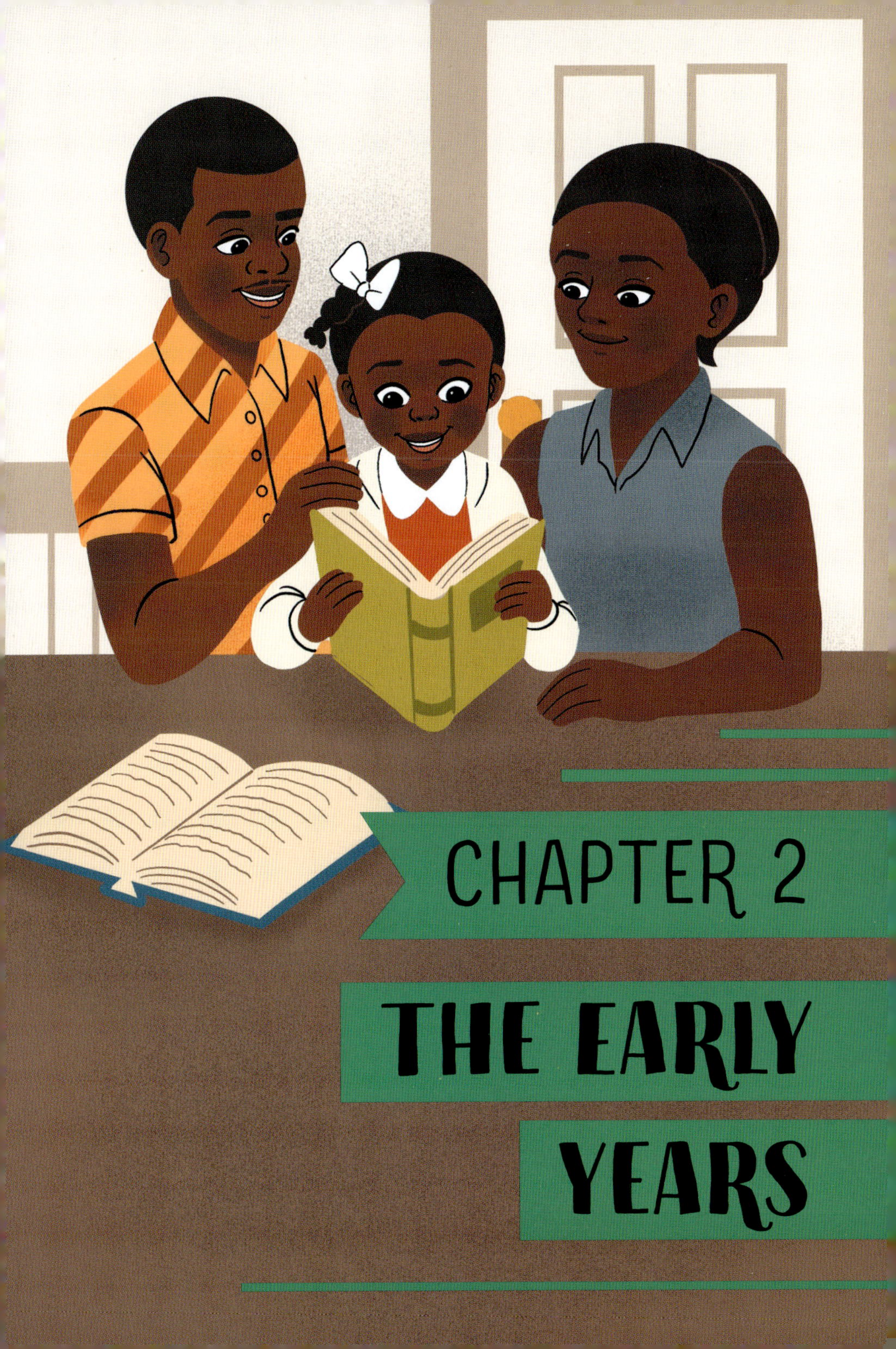

CHAPTER 2

THE EARLY YEARS

From the Farm to the City

Ruby grew up on a farm in Mississippi. Her parents and grandparents were farmers. They worked from sunup to sundown. Even though they worked very hard, they did not own the land that they farmed on. Instead, they worked under a **sharecropping** system. This meant that they lived and worked on someone else's land. Although they planted and picked all the crops, they were paid very little for their work.

MYTH & FACT

Myth: Sharecropping was a fair system.

Fact: Sharecropping was not fair. Many African Americans could not make enough money and were held back from owning land.

Many African Americans throughout the South worked as sharecroppers. The system was unfair and kept many African Americans in **poverty**. Even with these hardships, Ruby's childhood days were filled with happiness. She was especially close to her grandmother, who always showered her with love.

In 1958, Ruby's parents decided to move to New Orleans, Louisiana. They wanted to leave sharecropping behind and find better jobs. In the city, the family moved into a bigger house. They lived in a neighborhood with other

Black families. White people lived in separate neighborhoods. In their new home, Ruby's parents had four more children. Ruby became a busy big sister, often taking care of her brothers and sisters. She still found time to play. On summer days, she loved to play softball with her neighbors.

Her new life was great, but Ruby missed her grandparents. During the summers, she returned to Mississippi to visit them. She lived in the city, but she still loved the country.

Starting School

Soon it was time for Ruby to start kindergarten. She attended Johnson C. Lockett Elementary. Every morning, Ruby walked a few miles to get to school. She did not mind the walk, because her friends walked with her. There was an

The Bridges Family

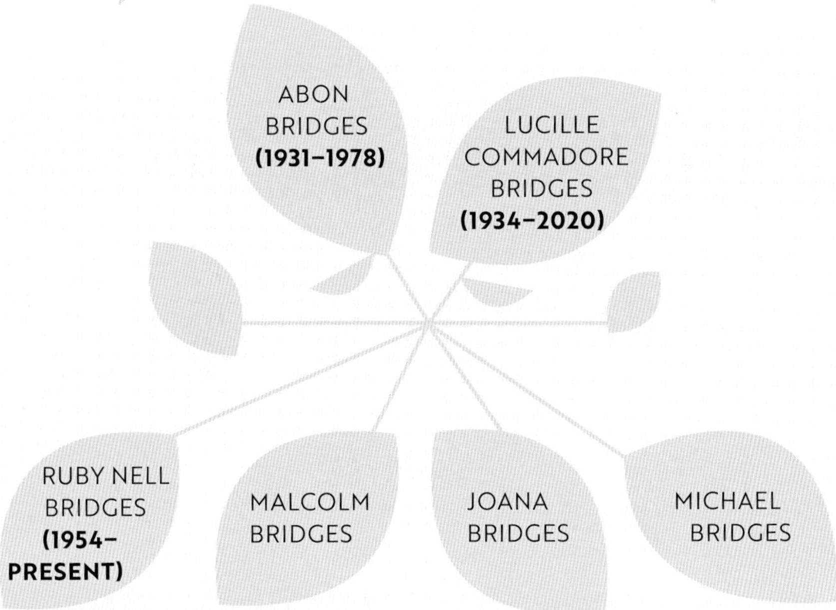

elementary school close to her house, but it was only for white children. Ruby did not know that she went to a segregated school. In fact, she loved her school. She adored her teacher Mrs. King, who made learning fun and easy.

By 1960, the government demanded that New Orleans **desegregate** schools. It was time for Black and white children to attend school together. But many people did not want integration. The school board created a very difficult test that Black children would have to pass in order to attend any white school. They hoped that no one would be able to pass the test and schools would stay segregated.

Ruby's parents decided that she should take the test. Ruby did not know that passing would

JUMP IN THE THINK TANK

Mrs. King made learning exciting for Ruby. Can you think of a teacher who makes learning fun for you? Write them a short note or letter thanking them for their work.

allow her to attend another school. She just tried her best to pass—and she did! She and five other Black children could **integrate** New Orleans public schools. Ruby was chosen to attend William Frantz, a white elementary school.

WHEN?

1958	1959	1960
Ruby and her family move to New Orleans, Louisiana.	Ruby starts kindergarten at Johnson C. Lockett Elementary.	Ruby passes the entrance test to attend a segregated school.

CHAPTER 3

THE FIRST DAY

A Difficult Decision

Ruby's parents had to make a difficult decision. If she decided to attend William Frantz Elementary, Ruby would lead the way for other children to integrate schools. She would also be the only African American child at her new school. Since the decision could impact other children, an organization called the **NAACP** reached out to Ruby and her parents. The NAACP is a large group created to help Black Americans with civil rights and social justice.

MYTH & FACT

MYTH: Schools were desegregated immediately after the *Brown v. Board of Education* ruling.

FACT: Even though the Supreme Court ruled that schools must desegregate, schools continued to resist. It took years for many of them, like William Frantz, to actually admit Black students.

It stands for "National Association for the Advancement of Colored People." The NAACP wanted to support Ruby in any way they could.

Ruby's father realized that attending school as the only African American child would be difficult. He did not want Ruby to be alone, and he feared that Ruby would never be treated equally. Ruby's mother wanted her to have a good education. She knew that *Brown v. Board of Education* made school segregation illegal. She believed it was time for integration to happen and that her daughter should be the first to break the barriers. It took some time, but eventually she convinced Ruby's father.

Once it was decided that Ruby should attend the school, the family started working with the NAACP. At first, the school tried to stop Ruby from attending. For a while, Ruby continued to attend her segregated school. After three months, Ruby was set to start at William Frantz Elementary in November.

JUMP -IN THE- THINK TANK

Think about the decision that Ruby's parents had to make. Have you ever had to make a difficult decision? How did it make you feel?

November 14, 1960, was picked as her first day of school.

Making an Entrance

When Ruby got ready for her first day in her new school, she had a brand-new dress and new shoes. Everything seemed to be going great!

Ruby and her mom rode to school with two men. As soon as they turned on to the street of her school, Ruby noticed barricades. Was today **Mardi Gras**? Ruby burst with excitement. New Orleans during Mardi Gras was a wonderful time! But something was different. The crowd did not seem like they were catching beads or celebrating. The two men in the front seat looked very serious. The men told Ruby and her mom to stay close and not turn around. Ruby did not know it yet, but the men were **federal marshals**. They were very important police officers sent by the president to protect Ruby at her new school.

> "All day long, white parents rushed into the office. They were upset. They were arguing and pointing at us."

When she stepped out of the car, Ruby heard people yelling. She could barely make out the words, but she knew that this was not Mardi Gras. The people yelled and pushed, making it difficult for her to enter her new school. The people yelling were protestors. They did not want Ruby to attend the all-white school. They did all they could to stop her from moving toward the door, but the marshals kept her moving forward.

Once inside, Ruby thought she would head straight to her new classroom. Instead, she was taken to the principal's office. The marshals instructed Ruby and her mother to sit in the office and not leave. A few moments later, Ruby noticed a flood of people walking in. One by one, they passed her and left with a child. They were white parents withdrawing their children from school. They did not want their children to attend the same school as an African American child. All day, Ruby watched parents take their kids out of school.

WHEN?

Ruby is assigned to William Frantz Elementary.

AUGUST 1960

Ruby begins William Frantz Elementary School.

NOVEMBER 14, 1960

CHAPTER 4

A CLASS OF ONE

Mrs. Henry

When Ruby arrived at school the next day, the crowd was even bigger and angrier. The marshals had to work harder to protect Ruby. They pushed through the crowd, and Ruby did

her best to ignore the screaming people. Once inside, she was escorted to an empty classroom. There were no other students, just Ruby. A woman introduced herself as Mrs. Henry. Mrs. Henry was from Boston, Massachusetts. She had traveled to New Orleans to teach at William Frantz because the other teachers refused to teach an African American child. At first, Ruby was unsure about Mrs. Henry and her new school. Even though Ruby's mother stayed by her side, she felt alone without any other students. Mrs. Henry was a white woman, and Ruby had never had a white teacher. But Mrs. Henry had a warm smile. This helped Ruby feel a little more comfortable.

JUMP IN THE THINK TANK

Mrs. Henry made Ruby feel more comfortable by being kind. Can you think of a time when someone made you feel more comfortable just by smiling? How often do you smile?

The second day went a little better than the first day.

A New Routine

On the third day of school, Ruby's mother let her know she could not stay with her in school anymore. Ruby would have to go to school alone. The crowd was still there, but the marshals were there, too. They walked Ruby into school and stayed with her throughout the day. Mrs. Henry always had a big smile, and she was always ready to teach Ruby.

MYTH & FACT

MYTH: No one at William Frantz Elementary wanted to desegregate the school.

FACT: Multiple parents were against segregation, and they made sure to keep their children in school after Ruby joined.

Mrs. Henry loved teaching Ruby, and she loved how the two of them were there for each other when no one else at the school was. Soon, Mrs. Henry and Ruby were good friends.

There were other students at the school, but Ruby never saw them. Pam Foreman's parents believed that segregation was wrong. They did not take Pam out of school. The Gabrielles also did not take their child Yolanda out of school. The families that chose to keep their kids at William Frantz also had to deal with the angry protestors. Ruby did not know Yolanda or Pam. The other kids were kept separate from her.

WHEN?

Mrs. Henry moves from Boston to New Orleans to teach Ruby.

1960

Peaceful protests, called sit-ins, begin in Atlanta.

1960

Freedom Rides protest buses that are still segregated.

MAY **1961**

CHAPTER 5

STAYING STRONG

All Eyes on Ruby

Ruby settled into her new school, but there were still protestors outside every day. The angry crowd moved through the city, starting violence in other neighborhoods. The riots lasted for many days. The protests also affected Ruby's family. Her father lost his job, and other New Orleans residents treated her mother poorly. Her parents could not shop for groceries without being **harassed**. Her grandparents even lost their farm in Mississippi. On many nights, Ruby's neighbors took turns guarding her house. They wanted to make sure that the protestors did not harm the Bridges family any more than they already had.

Although some people made it hard for the family, others supported Ruby's courageous decision. The family often received letters from people near and far. These letters were from people who were excited that Ruby was integrating the school. A few famous people—like First Lady Eleanor Roosevelt—sent letters telling the Bridges family how much they wanted Ruby to succeed.

People also sent money to support the family. The money was sent to Ruby, but she shared it with her siblings. Dr. Robert Coles was a child **psychologist**. He spent his time studying

and learning about children's brains and emotions. He decided to talk with Ruby about her feelings. **Counseling** helped her deal with the angry protestors. Ruby remained strong, but sometimes she missed her old life. She had nightmares about the protestors, and she was lonely. Ruby would often hide her lunch, because she hoped she would get a chance to go to the cafeteria. She longed to play and eat lunch with the other children.

MYTH & FACT

MYTH: Doctors only help if your body is feeling sick.

FACT: Psychologists are doctors that focus on the brain and emotions. They can help their patients when they are dealing with things that are difficult and affect their mental health.

Integration at Last

A few months into the school year, Mrs. Henry convinced some of the other parents to let their children join her classroom. Ruby was finally learning with other first graders. She was no longer lonely.

She especially enjoyed recess. During this time, she would play with her new classmates. One day, a classmate refused to play with her. When Ruby asked him why, he told her it was because she was Black.

She was hurt. She soon realized that all the protestors had been yelling about the color of her skin. Was that the reason that she had been in class alone? Many things started to make sense. Ruby knew that nothing was wrong with her skin. Her parents reminded her every

JUMP IN THE THINK TANK

Can you imagine how lonely Ruby felt? Can you imagine going to school and not being able to see your friends? What are some things you enjoy doing at school with your friends?

day that she was perfect just the way she was. Those who did not like her were wrong. One classmate did not like her because of her skin color, but many others loved her. She decided to ignore the hatred.

> "At that moment, it all made sense to me. I finally realized that **everything happened** because I was Black."

Ruby ended the year with perfect attendance and perfect grades.

Over the summer, Ruby was a little nervous about second grade. Would she be attending a new school? Would she be by herself in the classroom again?

Ruby found out she would be returning to William Frantz. When she arrived at school that fall, she noticed there were no protestors.

She got ready to head to her old classroom, but a teacher directed her to a different room. Ruby walked into her new second grade classroom and noticed there were both white children and other Black children, just like her. Ruby Bridges had successfully integrated William Frantz Elementary.

Ruby was happy, but she could not celebrate. Mrs. Henry was not there. Ruby's first grade teacher had gone back to Boston, Massachusetts. Ruby didn't get a chance to tell Mrs. Henry how much she appreciated her.

WHEN?

Mrs. Henry moves back to Boston.

SUMMER 1961

Ruby begins second grade.

SEPTEMBER 1961

The March on Washington takes place.

1963

The Civil Rights Act of 1964 is passed.

1964

CHAPTER 6

BECOMING AN ACTIVIST

All Grown Up

Ruby continued going to school at William Frantz Elementary. Every year, there were more African American kids in her class. By attending William Frantz, Ruby showed the world that segregation must end. Ruby made history.

Her courage inspired many people, including multiple artists. Famous American artist Norman Rockwell painted a very well-known picture of Ruby surrounded by protestors. Today, the painting is displayed in the White House.

Writer John Steinbeck also wrote about Ruby's experience in one of his books, called *Travels with Charley*.

As a young adult, Ruby's life looked like the life of any other teenager. She graduated high school and decided to become a travel agent. She married a man named Malcolm Hall and became a mother to four sons.

In 1990, Ruby returned to William Frantz Elementary to volunteer. She helped students and parents in the after-school program. She loved the work and found that being at William Frantz connected her with the past—a past that had changed history. While she was working at the school, Dr. Robert Coles published a book about Ruby's life. *The Story of Ruby Bridges* (different from this book!) introduced Ruby's story to children of all ages.

JUMP —IN THE— THINK TANK

Today, Ruby continues to give back and tell people her story. Do you know an important story that needs to be told? Maybe you should write the story down or tell someone.

MYTH & FACT

Myth: Once schools were integrated, racial equality was achieved.

Fact: Integrating schools was a huge step toward equality, but there is still a lot of work to be done. Organizations and activists all over the country (and the world!) still work hard today to ensure every person is treated equally.

The Ruby Bridges Foundation

Ruby continued to find ways to help the students at William Frantz and other schools in the New Orleans community. In 1999, she started the Ruby Bridges Foundation. The foundation aimed to spread **equality** and teach tolerance. She wrote three award-winning books about her childhood and desegregating William Frantz. Today, Ruby continues to travel the country talking about her time as a student at William Frantz and telling the world how courage can change history.

> "**Racism** is a grown-up disease, and we **must stop** using our children to spread it."

WHEN?

Norman Rockwell paints *The Problem We All Live With.*

1964

Ruby graduates from Francis T. Nicholls High School.

1972

Ruby marries Malcolm Hall.

1984

Ruby returns to William Frantz as a volunteer.

1990

Dr. Coles publishes *The Story of Ruby Bridges.*

1995

Ruby starts the Ruby Bridges Foundation.

1999

CHAPTER 7

SHARING HER STORY

A Special Reunion

As an adult, Ruby started traveling around the world, telling her story. She was often invited to talk about her experience. Ruby always talked about the protestors, but she also mentioned Mrs. Henry. Ruby and Mrs. Henry had not talked in many years. Mrs. Henry had moved back north to raise her family away from the violence and segregation of New Orleans. Ruby and Mrs. Henry had not stayed in touch, but Mrs. Henry never forgot Ruby. She always remembered how strong Ruby had been. She even kept a photo of Ruby.

> "I had never seen a white teacher before, but Mrs. Henry was the **nicest teacher** I ever had."

One day, Mrs. Henry discovered Ruby's book. She immediately contacted the publisher. She wanted to find Ruby and let her know how proud she was! In 1996, Ruby was invited to meet up with Mrs. Henry on *The Oprah Winfrey Show*.

When they finally saw each other again, Mrs. Henry and Ruby hugged tightly. Ruby remembered how Mrs. Henry's warm smile made a difference, and Mrs. Henry recalled

JUMP IN THE THINK TANK

Can you imagine how Ruby felt when she saw Mrs. Henry again? Have you ever been reunited with a friend or family member after a long time apart? How did you feel?

how resilient Ruby had been. The two continue to keep in touch, and they even travel and do book signings together.

Ruby's Legacy

Throughout her life, Ruby has continued to share her story. Her work reminds the world that segregation and racism have always been wrong. She has published books, visited schools, and received all kinds of awards, including the Presidential Citizens Medal. She even went to Washington, DC, to visit the White House. In 2014, Ruby was honored with a statue in front of William Frantz Elementary.

Today, when Ruby talks about her experience, she recalls how the protestors angrily stood

outside of her school. But she also teaches about those who helped her.

We are still dealing with many of the same issues that Ruby faced. Racism and segregation

continue to exist. Black people in the United States still face violence and inequality. But Ruby shows us that no matter how young or old you are, you can change the world.

WHEN?

1996 Ruby and Mrs. Henry reunite on Oprah's show.

1999 Ruby publishes *Through My Eyes*.

2001 Ruby receives the Presidential Citizens Medal.

2009 Ruby publishes *Ruby Bridges Goes to School*.

2014 William Frantz Elementary honors Ruby with a statue.

CHAPTER 8

SO . . . WHO IS RUBY BRIDGES?

Challenge Accepted!

Did you enjoy learning about Ruby? If so, let's test your knowledge in a little who, what, when, where, why, and how quiz. Feel free to look back in the text to find the answers if you need to, but try to remember first!

1 **Where was Ruby born?**

→ A New Orleans, Louisiana
→ B Washington, DC
→ C Tylertown, Mississippi
→ D Boston, Massachusetts

2 **How did Ruby initially feel about attending a new school?**

→ A Angry
→ B Scared
→ C Excited
→ D Sad

3 **Who is Mrs. Henry?**

→ A Ruby's mother
→ B Ruby's teacher
→ C A famous painter
→ D Ruby's doctor

4 **What is the NAACP?**

→ A The New Orleans school board
→ B A branch of US government
→ C A legal ruling
→ D A civil rights organization

5 **What is the name of Ruby's new elementary school?**

→ A William Frantz
→ B William Lockett
→ C Francis T. Nicholls
→ D Francis T. Harvey

6 **What year did Ruby integrate her school?**

- A 1957
- B 1958
- C 1959
- D 1960

7 **Who is Dr. Robert Coles?**

- A A Supreme Court judge
- B A college professor
- C A child psychologist
- D One of Ruby's teachers

8 **What is *Brown v. Board of Education*?**

- A The Supreme Court ruling that made segregating schools illegal
- B The NAACP policy to help Black students
- C The policy requiring entrance exams for Black students to enter white schools
- D The protest against ending school segregation

9 Who was Norman Rockwell and what did he do for Ruby?

→ A A writer who wrote about Ruby's life

→ B An artist who painted Ruby going to school

→ C A journalist who reported on Ruby's life

→ D A counselor who helped Ruby through school

10 What is the Ruby Bridges Foundation?

→ A The foundation William Frantz started to teach kindness

→ B The foundation Ruby started to spread equality

→ C The foundation Ruby's mother started in her honor

→ D The foundation New Orleans started to teach respect

Answers: 1. C; 2. C; 3. B; 4. D; 5. A; 6. D; 7. C; 8. A; 9. B; 10. B

Our World

As a little girl, Ruby changed the world. Today, you can see the impact of her work everywhere.

→ Ruby Bridges has been the focus of many paintings and books. You can find her story at several museums, and there is even a Disney movie about her called *Ruby Bridges*. The movie chronicles Ruby's time at William Frantz.

→ Many people use Ruby's story to teach about equality and courage. Her story has inspired both kids and adults.

→ Ruby Bridges continues to use her foundation to promote equality through education by traveling the country and speaking about her experiences.

JUMP IN THE THINK TANK FOR MORE!

Now let's think a little deeper about Ruby Bridges and how she changed history.

→ How has Ruby's courage changed your life? Think about how different school would be if Ruby had not integrated William Frantz Elementary.

→ Ruby and Mrs. Henry continue to travel the world to help teach people about injustice. What are some ways that you can teach others about injustice and inequality at home?

→ Ruby had to be very brave to change history. How can you be braver every day? Remember—you may make history some day!

Glossary

activist: A person who works to bring about change for something they care very much about

civil rights: Basic rights that every person has under the laws of the government to be treated fairly and equally

counseling: Talking to a professional to get advice and work through one's problems

desegregate: To end laws, policies, or both that keep races apart

discrimination: The unfair treatment of a person or group of people, based on where they come from, what they look like, what religion they are, or if they are men or women

equality: When every person in a group has the same rights and opportunities

federal: Having to do with the central or national government of the United States. This is different from the government of each individual state.

harass: To trouble or bother

injustice: An act or behavior that's not fair, right, or equal

integrate: To end segregation

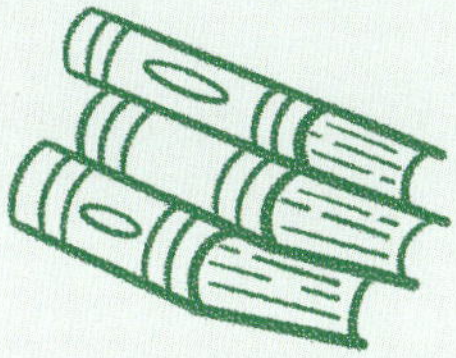

legacy: Something a person leaves behind that they are remembered for

Mardi Gras: A celebration that happens every year in New Orleans, Louisiana, and many other cities in the South; the festival includes lots of costumes and street parades, and it marks the beginning of the Christian season called Lent

marshal: A high-ranking law officer or official

NAACP: The National Association for the Advancement of Colored People: a civil rights organization founded to help gain equal social and civil rights for Black Americans

poverty: The state of being very poor

psychologist: An expert in human behavior and the brain who helps people by listening to them talk about their problems

racism: Discrimination against someone of a different race based on the belief that one's own race is superior

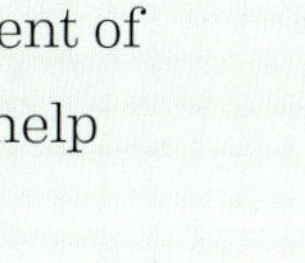

segregate: To separate people, usually based on their race or skin color

sharecropping: A system in which landowners allow farmers to use land in exchange for part of their harvest

Supreme Court: The highest court in the United States, made up of nine justices who have the power to hear and rule on all other state and local court cases; being on the Supreme Court is a lifelong job—you can't get fired

unconstitutional: When an action, law, or policy goes against the rights granted to every citizen

violence: The use of physical force to harm someone or something

Bibliography

Bridges, Ruby. *Ruby Bridges Goes to School*. New York: Scholastic, 2009.

Bridges, Ruby. *Through My Eyes*. New York: Scholastic Press, 1999.

Coles, Robert. *The Story of Ruby Bridges*. New York: Scholastic, 1995.

Devlin, Rachel. *A Girl Stands at the Door: The Generation of Young Women Who Desegregated America's Schools*. New York: Basic Books, 2018.

Palcy, Euzhan, dir. *Ruby Bridges*. Los Angeles, CA: Disney, 1998.

About the Author

ARLISHA NORWOOD is a historian, researcher, and social justice advocate. She received her PhD in history from Howard University. She has published several children's books, including *Black Heroes: A Black History Book for Kids: 51 Inspiring People from Ancient Africa to Modern-Day U.S.A.* She aims to convey her love of history through innovative and exciting methods.

About the Illustrator

KATIE CRUMPTON was born in South Carolina in 1992 but now lives in the Bay Area. She moved to California to attend the Academy of Art University and graduated with a bachelor's degree in illustration in 2016. She started drawing from a very young age and was too stubborn to stop.

Katie gets inspired by going on long walks, reading, watching movies, and playing video games. Animals, nature, magical themes, and spooky things are also creative fuel for her.

When Katie isn't drawing she's probably watching the Harry Potter movies for the umpteenth time, Hula-Hooping, creating music, or exploring a bookshop.

Katie is primarily a digital artist, because it's convenient and portable. She enjoys drawing whimsical, weird, and cute things that make her happy.

Katie likes listening to music or podcasts while she works. Her taste in music ranges from upbeat synth and pop to movie soundtracks and punk.